Bertha B Kauly

FLOWER

ARRANGEMENTS

TO COPY

Flower Arrangements to Copy

BY TAT SHINNO

ILLUSTRATED BY THE AUTHOR

Doubleday & Company, Inc.
Garden City, New York

Acknowledgment:

I am deeply indebted to Thelma L. King for cultivating, putting at my disposal, and listing the variety of plant materials appearing in these arrangements.

TAT SHINNO

Contents

FLOWER

ARRANGEMENTS

TO COPY

The Lure of Flower Arranging

How fortunate and wealthy we are to have such an abundance of plants and flowers growing about us! They bring into our lives, oftentimes unrealized by us, the constant message of perfection, wholeness, freshness, harmony, and contentment with life on this earth.

Some of us are so keenly aware of the charm of plants that we grow and care for them in our gardens. Others of us will court them by journeying to inspiring gardens, parks, and mountain areas to partake of their beauty. Thus, outdoors, plants give to each of us this message every day of the year. Indoors, where the walls of our rooms or the darkness of night separates us from this beauty, we use flower arrangements to keep our contact with this subtle quality. But plants and blossoms haphazardly arranged do not preserve this message. Such an arrangement will shout its annoyance at being mishandled and can set our nerves on edge. Yet there is no other form of art which is so eloquent in its expression nor so complete in its reward as an arrangement of flowers that preserves the plants' intrinsic beauty when rearranged for the home. A flower arrangement, being the only art form that can be created quickly and easily, allows us to enjoy seasonal changes indoors and keeps our lives constantly refreshed and inspired.

We should all have flower arrangements in our homes. A room that contains a fresh flower arrangement speaks of a family aware of the beauties of Nature and it helps to greet everyone graciously with its warmth and vitality.

The art of flower arranging is not gained by learning a style, nor in following set rules, but flower arranging becomes an art only when the beauty of the natural plant or blossom shines through a design controlled by rules. It takes but a little awareness and a little respect to learn what it is about plants and flowers in the garden that attracts our attention and admiration. Such flower arranging requires only a simple container, a proper flower holder, and living plant and flower materials. With these materials we can always enjoy the beauty of plants indoors.

For the busy homemaker, mother, interior decorator, and host and hostess who wish to immediately enjoy the charm of flowers well arranged, but have no time to learn the art of flower arranging, we have written this book. Select a design you like and copy it outright or adapt it.

Copying these designs will give you an arrangement executed with all the deftness acquired from years of study. No training is necessary. No knowledge of principles and rules is important because it is already applied for you in these designs. Each arrangement has been carefully executed in proper balance, texture combinations, and color harmony, and, above all, it preserves the intrinsic beauty of the flowers. Many styles and moods are included so that throughout the year you will find designs to fit your need.

The text is brief but gives all the pertinent points required to re-create each design. The container measurements are given so that you can gauge how small or large the finished design will be. These measurements also key you to the relative size of each plant material and should be referred to when you select a substitute container or flower material to preserve the over-all balance and interest. All plant materials in each arrangement are easily found at the same time of year and in the same locale.

A glossary of terms and things to know are included to clarify the procedure of arranging and explains the terms used in the description of the arrangements. First acquaint yourself with these terms and points of help.

Copying these designs will teach you the functional as well as the aesthetic value of flower arranging. It is hoped that the many different designs using the same plant material, the variety of designs created for the same container, and the manner in which containers and bases are used will stimulate your own creativity.

To know and use all the rules governing design, color combinations, and texture blends and to acquire the deftness of handling flower materials in creating a given effect require serious and dedicated study. True command of the art cannot be gained immediately. For the serious student of flower arranging who desires to know the whats, whens, wheres, whys, and hows of this art, the author has written a previous book, *Flower Arranging by Tat,* 1961, Tat's Inc., Walteria, California.

In the meantime use these designs and enjoy immediately the results as though you had studied flower arranging for many years.

Things to Know
for Copying These Designs

1   Harden all fresh plant materials before using. This is done by recutting their stems and putting them in deep water for at least an hour.

2   Split the stem end of woody or thick stems several times to make it easier for the needles of the kenzan to penetrate them.

3   Thin stems are made thicker by enclosing them in a hollow stem or binding another stem to it.

4   Weak stems can be supported by inserting a firm stem behind them and binding the two together with wire or floral tape.

5   Bamboo should be placed in water immediately after it is cut.

6   The water level in cup holders and containers should be checked each day.

7   Arrangements designed with no water feeding their stems are meant to be used for a special party. They can be kept fresh by misting them with water.

8   Any material with similiar structure, form, and color can be substituted for the variety used in each design.

9 Dimensions of the container are given to help in establishing the size of the design and accessories used.

10 Before beginning your arrangement, put water in your container.

11 Taper cut all stems that are used in Styrofoam, oasis, or fruit.

12 Acquaint yourself with each term in the glossary before you begin your design.

ANCHOR   To secure with floral clay.

BALANCE   Visual balance differing from physical balance.

BIZEN WARE   Ware made from the famous Bizen kilns in Japan.

CENTERPIECE   An arrangement to be placed in the center of a table and designed to be effective from all views.

COCO STICKS   Midribs taken from the coconut-palm leaf.

COMPOTE   A shallow bowl with a pedestal or foot.

CROSS STICKS   Short stems attached horizontally to the lower part of a stem. A cross stick braces itself against the inside of the vase to control the position of the stem. Cross sticks are either bound to the stem or slipped into a slit made in the stem.

CUP HOLDER   A shallow cup with a kenzan fitted within it. Cup holders are used when water is not used directly in the container or when a container is not watertight.

CUTOUT VASE   A vase with a portion or portions of its sides removed.

FLORAL CLAY   A special nonhardening clay made for flower-arranging use.

FLORAL TAPE   A waxed crepe paper that adheres to itself when stretched.

FROG BOWL   A container with a flower holder attached.

GLASS CHIPS   Small pieces of broken glass. These are available in many colors.

GLASS SLAG Chunks of glass. These are available in many sizes, shapes, and colors.

GLYCERINIZED Plant material treated with gylcerine.

HARDEN To fill the flower stem with water.

KENZAN A flower holder made with sharp needles embedded in either a plastic or a metal base. Kenzans with sharp brass needles set close together are recommended. They are available in such sizes as follow:
"Large" 3 to 4 inches in diameter.
"Medium" 2 to 3 inches in diameter.
"Small" 1 to 1½ inches in diameter.
"Tiny" ½ inch in diameter.

KIRI WOOD Wood native to Japan.

LINE—COMPLEX A stem that draws the eye in more than one direction, as done by the S line.

LINE—SIMPLE A stem that draws the eye in one direction, as done by a vertical line or the C line.

MATERIAL Items assembled to create a design.

MATTE Dull finish.

OASIS A spongelike synthetic foam that absorbs water and may be carved into shape. Flower stems are pierced directly into it.

PICKS Wire-attached pointed wooden sticks.

PLATEAUS Bases made in sets; each is a different size, and the plateaus are generally used stacked.

SANDSTONE   A sandy-surfaced ceramic ware.

STICKUM   A gummy tape that is adhesive on both sides. Used to secure Styrofoam, kenzans, figurines, etc. To remove it, use a petroleum-base solvent.

STONEWARE   A hard, heavy ceramic ware.

STYROFOAM   A plastic foam used as a holder for dry or artificial flower-stem control. Does not absorb water.

SUIBAN   A flat-bottomed shallow container finished with a blue or bluish inner glaze. It is used when a stream or pond, river, swamp, lake, etc., is to be a part of the arrangement.

SUNABACHI   A shallow (not more than 1½ inches in depth), flat-bottomed platter designed primarily for sandscapes.

TEMPLE VASE   A container of a specific design.

USUBATA   A bronze, Japanese classical container with a saucer top.

WIRE PICKS   Wire-attached pointed wooden sticks.

WOOD BURL SLAB   A section of a wood burl cut and polished.

Plant Substitution

The plant materials arranged in this book are easily grown outdoors in temperate climates. In areas of extreme temperatures they can be grown under controlled hothouse conditions. Some of the flowers, such as bird-of-paradise (*Strelitzia*) or peonies, both of which naturally belong to extreme climatic areas, are now available through your florist. I realize that many desirable flower-arranging plants such as lilacs, laurels, rhododendrons, phloxes, apple blossoms, dogwoods, stocks, freesias, galax, hyacinths, hostas, maples, anemones, mesquite, cacti, antherium, ginger, cannas, and many thousands more plants have not been included. Because of this, and because of the difficulty you may have in finding some of the materials in your area, I would like to make the following very simple suggestion to each person using this book.

It is not necessary for you to know the names of plants or their culture to enjoy flower arranging. Study the design and *capture* the feeling of the form, texture, size, and colors of the design. For instance, the lily-of-the-Nile (*Agapanthus*) is a single dramatic flower with distinct foliage. For a substitute, look around and use a flower of the lily family available to you. Where branches are used, substitute branch materials of similiar structure and foliage and utilize flowering shrubs and trees found in your area. In short, *simply use the various combinations of materials as suggestions for arranging materials you find near at hand.*

A plant list is included for those who desire to acquaint themselves further with the actual plant material used in the flower arrangements shown.

Plants used in the arrangements

ACACIA (*Acacia baileyana purpurea*) Evergreen tree. Needs temperate climate. Native of Australia.

AGAPANTHUS OR LILY-OF-THE-NILE (*Agapanthus umbellatus*) Evergreen perennial of tuberous rootstock. Half-hardy. Native of the Cape of Good Hope.

AGATHEA or FELICIA or BLUE MARGUERITE (*Felicia amelloides*) Hardy perennial. Native of South Africa.

ALGERIAN IVY (*Hedera canariensis*) Hardy evergreen vine. Native to the Azores and the Canaries.

ALYSSUM, SWEET (*Lobularia maritima*) Very hardy perennial herb. Native of Europe.

AMARYLLIS (*Amaryllis belladonna*) Lily that must be grown indoors except in temperate climate. Native of South Africa.

ANGEL-WING BEGONIA (*Begonia rex*) Succulent-stemmed perennial needing winter protection. Native of Asia.

ARALIA (*Fatsia japonica*) Evergreen tropical shrub. Native of Japan.

ASPARAGUS FERN (*Asparagus plumosus*) Evergreen, woody climbing vine. Needs temperate climate. Native of South Africa.

ASPARAGUS VINE (*Asparagus falcatus*) Giant tropical evergreen vine. Native of Ceylon and South Africa.

ASPIDISTRA (*Aspidistra elatior*) Thick-rooted perennial herb. Will accept very poor growing conditions. Native of southern China.

AUSTRALIAN BRAKE FERN (*Pteris tremula*) Evergreen fern. Needs temperate climate. Native of Tasmania.

AZALEA (*Rhododendron*) Both evergreen and deciduous types. Native of North America, China, and Japan.

BABY GLADIOLUS (*Gladiolus colvillei*) Cormous plant. Developed from stock native of South Africa.

BALLOON-VINE (*Cardiospermum halicacabum*) Annual vine. Needs temperate climate. Native of tropical America.

BARBERRY (*Berberis thunbergi*) Deciduous shrub. Native of Japan.

BEARDED IRIS Hardy perennial rhizome plant. Hybridized in the United States.

BIRD-OF-PARADISE (*Strelitzia reginae*) Evergreen tropical shrub of twining habit. Native of North America.

BITTERSWEET (*Celastrus scandens*) Hardy deciduous perennial. Native of South Africa.

BLACK ALDER (*Alnus glutinosa*) Hardy deciduous tree Native of North America.

Blue-Eyed Grass (*Sisyrinchium*) Grasslike perennial. Native of North America.

Bush Morning Glory (*Convolvulus cneorum*) Small hardy evergreen shrub. Native of southern Europe.

Buttercup (*Ranunculus repens*) Wild flower. Native of North America.

Calla Lily (*Zantedeschia aethiopica*) Evergreen tuberous-rooted plant. Needs temperate climate. Native of South Africa.

Camellia (*Camellia japonica*) Evergreen shrub. Needs protection where winters are severe. Native of China and Japan.

Candytuft (*Iberis sempervirens*) White perennial creeping evergreen. Native of Spain.

(*Iberis umbellata*) Annual in many colors. Native of Spain.

Carnation (*Dianthus caryophyllus*) Common carnation. Hardy perennial. Native of South Europe and India.

Catalpa (*Catalpa bignonioides*) Deciduous tree native of North America and Asia. Hardy in extreme temperatures.

Cat-tails (*Typha augustifolia*) Aquatic plant. Native of North America.

Celosia or Cockscomb (*Celosia argentea cristata*) Hardy annual. Native of the East Indies.

CHINESE GARLIC Hardy herb.

CHRYSANTHEMUM (*Chrysanthemum morifolium*) Perennial herbaceous plant. Native of Japan.

CLIVIA or KAFIR LILY (*Clivia miniata*) Tender bulb. Native of Natal.

COCKSCOMB (*Celosia argentea cristata*) Hardy annual. Native of the East Indies.

CORREA or AUSTRALIAN FUCHSIA (*Correa pulchella*) Evergreen shrub. Native of Australia.

CRESS (*Plectranthus*) Evergreen creeper. Native of Australia. Subtropical and tropical climates required.

CYMBIDIUM Decorative epiphytic orchid. Needs mild climate. Native of the mountains of Asia.

DAFFODIL (*Narcissus*) Hardy bulb. Native of Europe.

DAHLIA Perennial, herbaceous, tuberous plant. Native of Mexico.

DAYLILY (*Hemerocallis*). Fleshy-rooted hardy perennial. Chinese ancestry.

DIANTHUS or PINK (*Dianthus chinensis heddewigii*) Hardy herb of Chinese ancestry.

DUSTY MILLER (*Centaurea cineraria*) Hardy evergreen perennial. Native of Sicily.

DUTCH IRIS (*Iris xiphium*) Hardy bulb. Spanish, Portuguese, and North African ancestry.

ENGLISH HOLLY (*Ilex aquifolium fertile*) Evergreen shrub. Likes cold climate. European origin.

EPIDENDRUM or MEXICAN ORCHID Epiphytic tropical orchid. Native of Central America.

EQUISETUM or HORSETAIL (*Equisetum hyemale*) Perennial grass. Native of North America.

ESCALLONIA (*Escallonia organensis*) Evergreen shrub. Not hardy where winter is severe. Native of South America.

ESTHER REED DAISY (*Chrysanthemum maximum*) Hardy perennial. Hybridized in the United States.

FERNS

AUSTRALIAN BRAKE (*Pteris tremula*) Evergreen. Needs temperate climate. Native of Tasmania.

DELTA MAIDENHAIR (*Adiantum cuneatum*) Tender, mostly a greenhouse plant. Native of Brazil.

LEATHERWOOD (*Dryopteris marginalis*) Hardy evergreen. Native of eastern North America.

FLOWERING ALMOND (*Prunus glandulosa sinensis*) Deciduous shrub with pink flowers.

(*Prunus glandulosa alboplena*) Deciduous shrub with white flowers.

FLOWERING PEACH (*Prunus persica flore pleno*) Deciduous flowering tree. Hardy to 10 degrees below. Chinese ancestry.

FOUNTAIN GRASS (*Pennisetum ruppeli*) Perennial grass. Native of the tropics.

FRANCOA or MAIDEN'S-WREATH (*Francoa ramosa*) Hardy perennial herb. Native of Chile.

FRENCH MARIGOLD (*Tagetes patula*) Annual. French ancestry.

FUCHSIA Evergreen shrub. Needs temperate climate. Hybridized in the United States.

GAILLARDIA or PINCUSHION DAISY (*Gaillardia aristata*) Hardy perennial.

GERANIUM Evergreen perennial. Not hardy in cold climate. Native of the Canary Islands.

> COMMON (LADY WASHINGTON) (*Pelargonium domesticum*).
>
> NUTMEG (*Pelargonium odoratissimum*).
>
> ORNAMENTAL (*Pelargonium hortorum*).
>
> PEPPERMINT (*Pelargonium tomentosum*).
>
> ROSE (*Pelargonium graveolens*).
>
> PELARGONIUM GRANDIFLORA Geranium with deeply lobed leaves.

GERBERA or TRANSVAAL DAISY (*Gerberia jamesonii*) Hardy perennial. Native of Africa.

GIANT BAMBOO (*Sinocalamus oldhami*) Evergreen woody grass. Hardy to 20 degrees. Native of the Orient.

18

GLADIOLUS   Hardy cormous plant. Native of South Africa.

>   GARDEN (*Gladiolus hortulanus*).

>   BABY (*Gladiolus colvillei*).

>   TRISTIS (*Gladiolus tristis concolor*).

GLORIOSA DAISY or PINWHEEL DAISY (*Rudbeckia hirta Burpeeii*) Annual or perennial. Hardy to zero weather.

GOLDEN BAMBOO (*Phyllostachys aurea*)   Evergreen woody grass. Hardy. Drought resistant. Native of the Orient.

HAHN IVY (*Hedera helix Hahnii*)   Small-leafed evergreen vine. Tropical origin.

ICELAND POPPY (*Papaver nudicaule*)   Hardy perennial herb. Hybridized in the United States.

INDIAN CHIEF BEGONIA (*Begonia semperflorens*) Succulent herb. Native of the warm regions of the earth.

INNOMINATA IRIS   Hardy evergreen. Native of the West Coast of the United States.

IRIS

>   BEARDED   Hardy perennial plant. Hybridized in the United States.

>   DUTCH (*Iris xiphium*)   Hardy bulb of Spanish, Portuguese, and North African ancestry. Hybridized in Europe.

>   INNOMINATA   Hardy evergreen. Native of the West Coast of the United States.

IRIS (Cont'd)

> JAPANESE (*Iris japonica*) Needs mild climate. Native of Japan.

> SPURIA Hardy perennial. Native of Europe and Asia.

JAPANESE IRIS (*Iris japonica*) Needs mild climate.

JAPANESE LILIES (*Lillum speciosum album*) White flower. Adaptable to many climates.

> (*Lillum speciosum rubrum*) Pink flower. Adaptable to many climates.

JAPANESE RICE-PAPER PLANT (*Tetrapanax papyriferum*) Evergreen shrub. Hardy to 25 degrees. Native of China and Formosa.

JOHNNY JUMP-UP (*Viola tricolor hortensis*) Hardy annual. Grows wild in the United States. Native of Europe.

KALANCHOE (*Kalanchoe coccinea*) Perennial herb. Popular greenhouse plant. Native of the tropics and South Africa.

LADY WASHINGTON GERANIUM. See GERANIUMS.

LEATHERWOOD FERN (*Dryopteris marginalis*) Hardy evergreen. Native of eastern North America.

LEMON (*Citrus limonia*) Small evergreen semitropical tree. Injured by frost.

LILY-OF-THE-NILE (*Agapanthus umbellatus*) Half-hardy perennial evergreen. Native of South Africa.

LIRIOPE (*Liriope muscari*) Evergreen perennial grass. Native of Japan and China.

LOQUAT (*Eriobotrya japonica*) Subtropical evergreen tree. Native of Japan.

LUNARIA, HONESTY, MOONWART, or SATIN-FLOWER (*Lunaria annua*) Hardy annual plant.

MAGNOLIA (*Magnolia grandiflora*) Large evergreen tree. Native of the southern United States.

SAUCER or PURPLE LILY (*Magnolia soulangeana*) Deciduous tree or shrub. Native of the Orient.

MAIDENHAIR FERN, DELTA (*Adiantum cuneatum*) Tender, mostly a greenhouse plant. Native of Brazil.

MARGUERITE (*Chrysanthemum frutescens*) Hardy perennial herbaceous plant. Native of the Canary Islands.

MEADOW SILK GRASS Perennial grass. Native of the western United States.

MEXICAN ORCHID (*Epidendrum*) Epiphytic tropical orchid. Native of Central America.

MONTEREY PINE (*Pinus radiata*) Evergreen tree. Native of California.

MORAEA IRIS (*Moraea iridioides*) Perennial evergreen. Native of South Africa. Naturalized in California and Florida.

MYRTLE (*Myrtus communis*) Hardy evergreen shrub. Native of the Mediterranean region and western Asia.

NARCISSUS or DAFFODIL Hardy bulb with European ancestry.

NASTURTIUM (*Tropaeolum*) Hardy annual. Native of Peru and Chile.

NATAL PLUM (*Carissa grandiflora*) Evergreen shrub. Native of Natal and South Africa.

NEW ZEALAND FLAX, VARIEGATED and BRONZE (*Phormium tenax*) Evergreen perennial. Native of New Zealand.

NUTMEG GERANIUM (*Pelargonium odoratissimum*) Evergreen perennial weed.

ORNAMENTAL GERANIUM. See GERANIUM.

PEACH (*Prunus persica*) Deciduous fruit tree. Hardy to 15 degrees below zero. Native of China.

PEPPERMINT GERANIUM (*Pelargonium tomentosum*) Evergreen perennial. Native to the Canary Islands.

PETUNIA (*Petunia hybrida*) Hardy annual or perennial. Much hybridized in the United States.

PINEAPPLE GUAVA (*Feijoa sellowiana*) Large hardy evergreen shrub. Native of tropical America.

PINWHEEL GLORIOSA DAISY. See GLORIOSA DAISY.

PITTOSPORUM CRASSIFOLIUM Tall evergreen shrub. Requires temperate climate. Native of New Zealand.

PITTOSPORUM RHOMBIFOLIUM Tall shrub or small tree. Evergreen. Native of Queensland, Australia.

PLUMED CELOSIA. (*Celosia plumosa*) Hardy annual. Native of the East Indies.

POINCIANA or BIRD-OF-PARADISE BUSH (*Poinciana gilliesii*) Shrub or small tree. Will not accept freezing temperatures. Native of tropical regions.

POMEGRANATE (*Punica granatum*) Deciduous shrub or tree. Tropical or subtropical. Native of Iran.

PURPLE ACACIA. See ACACIA.

PURPLE-LEAF PLUM (*Prunus pissardii*) Deciduous tree. Hardy in most of the United States.

PUSSY WILLOW (*Salix discolor*) Deciduous tree or shrub. Very hardy. Native of eastern North America.

PYRACANTHA or FIRETHORN (*Pyracantha P. K. Stribling*) Hardy evergreen shrub. Native of southern Europe and Asia Minor.

QUAKING GRASS (*Briza*) Perennial grass. Native of the Old World and Mexico.

RAPHIOLEPIS or INDIA HAWTHORN (*Raphiolepis indica rosea*) Needs mild climate. Killed at o degrees. Native to southern China and Japan.

ROSE GERANIUM. See GERANIUM.

ROSES   Deciduous shrubs. Hardy. Grown throughout the world.

HYBRID TEAS   One large flower to each stem.

FLORIBUNDA   Medium-sized flowers in thick clusters.

POLYANTHA   Very small flowers in thick bunches.

SAUCER MAGNOLIA (*Magnolia soulangeana*)   Deciduous tree or shrub. Native of the Orient. Grows throughout the United States.

SAXIFRAGE (*Bergenia ligulata*)   Evergreen perennial. Native of the Himalayas.

SCABIOSA or PINCUSHION-FLOWER (*Scabiosa atropurpurea*)   Hardy annual. Native of Europe, Asia, and Africa.

SCILLA or SPANISH BLUEBELL (*Scilla campanulata* or *hispanica*)   Hardy bulb. Native of Spain and Portugal.

SEA-OATS (*Uniola paniculata*)   Perennial grass. Native of the sanddunes of the southern United States and will grow as far north as Canada.

SILVER DOLLAR EUCALYPTUS (*Eucalyptus polyanthemos*)   Evergreen tree. Hardy in extreme temperatures. Native of Australia.

SPANISH BROOM (*Spartium junceum*)   Hardy. Likes dry climate. Native of southern Europe.

SPARAXIS TRICOLOR or WAND-FLOWER   Hardy bulb. Native of South Africa.

SPIDER LILY (*Lycoris aurea*) Bulbous plant. Native of China and Japan.

SPIRAL EUCALYPTUS (*Eucalyptus pulverulenta*) Evergreen tree. Native of Australia and Malayan regions.

(SPURIA) IRIS or BUTTERFLY IRIS Tall hardy evergreen. Native of central and south Europe.

STATICE or SEA LAVENDER (*Limonium latifolium*) Perennial. Native of Russia, Bulgaria, and the Caucasus.

STOCK (*Mathiola incana*) Annual. Native of the Mediterranean region.

STRAWBERRY GUAVA (*Psidium cattleianum*) Subtropical evergreen shrub. Thrives above 15 degrees. Native of tropical America.

SUCCULENTS Fleshy plants. Like warm climates, but some are hardy in latitude of New York. Natives of Mexico, South America, and South Africa.

SUN CAMELLIA (*Camellia sasanqua*) Evergreen shrub. Needs winter protection. Native of China and Japan.

TIGER LILY (*Lilium tigrinum*) Perennial bulb. Hardy wild orange lily. Native of China and Japan.

TRANSVAAL DAISY (*Gerberia jamesonii*) Hardy perennial. Native of Africa.

TRISTIS (*Gladiolus tristis concolor*) Baby gladiolus. Hardy south of Washington State.

25

TWISTED JUNIPER (*Juniperus chinensis torulosa*) Large hardy evergreen shrub. Native of China, Mongolia, and Japan.

UMBRELLA PLANT (*Cyperus alternifolius*) Aquatic plant. Native of the Lord Howe Islands.

VIOLA (*Viola cornuta*) Hardy annual. Native of the Old World.

WALLFLOWER (*Cheiranthus cheiri*) Hardy annual. Native of southern Europe.

WATSONIA Half-hardy bulb. Native of South Africa.

WILLOW Deciduous hardy tree. Native of the Northern Hemisphere.

    CORKSCREW (*Salix*).

    PUSSY (*Salix discolor*).

YARROW (*Achillea taggetea*) Native weed under cultivation.

Some additional plants for effective arranging

ABELIA (*Abelia grandiflora*)   Half-deciduous shrub. Needs temperate climate. Native of China and Mexico.

ALTHAEA or ROSE-OF-SHARON (*Althea frutex*)   Hardy deciduous shrub. Native of the Near East.

ANCHUSA or SUMMER-FORGET-ME-NOT (*Brunnera macrophylia*)   Biennial herbaceous plant. Hardy. Native of North America.

APRICOT (*Prunus armeniaca*)   Hardy deciduous fruit tree. Native of Russia.

ASTER or WONDER OF STAFA (*Aster frikartii*)   Perennial. Native of both hemispheres.

AUCUBA or GOLD-DUST PLANT (*Aucuba japonica variegata*) Hardy evergreen shrub. Needs winter protection. Native of Japan.

BILLBERGIA (*Billbergia nutans*)   Perennial, grasslike air plants. Native of southern Brazil.

BIRCH (*Betula alba*)   Hardy deciduous tree. Native of Europe.

BLUEBELL FLOWER (*Campanula*) Hardy perennial herb. Native of North America.

BLEEDING HEART (*Dicentra spectabilis*) Hardy perennial. Native of Japan.

BORAGE (*Borago officinalis*) Annual herb. Native of Germany.

BOTTLEBRUSH (*Melaleuca*) Evergreen shrub. Hardy to 15 degrees. Native of Australia.

BRAZILIAN PEPPER (*Schinus terebinthifolius*) Evergreen tree. Hardy to 20 degrees. Native of Brazil.

BRIDAL WREATH (*Spiraea vanhouttei*). Hardy deciduous shrub. Native of temperate regions of the Northern Hemisphere.

CAPE MARIGOLD (*Dimorphotheca*) Daisy. Perennial shrub. Native of South Africa.

CHINESE ORCHID (*Bletilla striata*) Tuberous perennial. Hardy except in extreme cold. Native of China.

CLOVER (*Polygonum capitatum*) Perennial ground cover.

COCCULUS (*Cocculus laurifolius*) Very hardy large evergreen shrub. Native of Asia.

COLUMBINE (*Aquilegia longissima*) Hardy perennial. Native of North America.

CORAL BELLS (*Heuchera sanguinea*) Evergreen perennial. Native of northwestern America.

28

COROKIA COTONEASTER   Evergreen shrub. Hardy in light frost. Native of Australia and New Zealand.

COTONEASTER (*Cotoneaster parneyi*) Hardy evergreen shrub. Deciduous species hardy in all zones. Native of the temperate regions of Europe, North Africa, and Asia.

CUP-OF-GOLD VINE (*Solandra guttata*) Evergreen vine. Will not stand cold. Native of tropical America.

DELPHINIUM, PACIFIC GIANTS   Extremely hardy perennial. Parent plants native of temperate regions of North America.

FORSYTHIA or GOLDEN BELL (*Forsythia spectabilis*) Hardy deciduous shrub. Native of Asia.

HOLLYHOCK (*Althaea rosea*) Hardy perennial. Hybridized in the United States.

IXIA or AFRICAN CORN LILY (*Ixia columellaris*).   Half-hardy bulb. Native of South Africa.

JAPANESE MAPLE (*Acer palmatum*)   Deciduous tree. Needs protection from the elements.

KUMQUAT (*Fortunella margarita*)   Small evergreen tree. Native of the Orient.

LANTANA (*Lantana camara*) Evergreen shrub. Hardy to 24 degrees. Native of North America.

LEOPARD PLANT (*Aureo-maculatas*) Evergreen perennial. Native of China.

LEPTOSPERMUM, ROSE PINK POMPON Evergreen shrub. Needs warm climate. Native of Australia and New Zealand.

LILAC (*Syringa vulgaris*) Deciduous shrub. Needs cold winters. Native of southeastern Europe.

LOUISIANA IRIS Adaptable to many climates. Native of southern United States.

MELALEUCA or BOTTLE-BRUSH (*Melaleuca*) Evergreen shrub. Hardy to 15 degrees. Native of Australia.

MOCK ORANGE (*Philadelphus coronarius*) Very hardy deciduous shrub. Hybrid with European ancestry.

MONDO GRASS (*Mondo japonicus*) Perennial grass from the Orient.

NANDINA or HEAVENLY BAMBOO or SACRED BAMBOO (*Nandina domestica*) Hardy evergreen shrub. Can stand freezing temperatures. Native of China and Japan.

NERINE (*Nerine sarniensis*) Lily from South Africa.

PAMPAS GRASS (*Cortaderia selloana*) Giant ornamental perennial grass. Native of Argentina and southern Brazil.

PARROT TULIP (*Tulipa*) Bulb introduced into Europe from Turkey.

PEONY (*Paeonia*) Perennial, hardy with cold winters. Native of China and Japan.

PITTOSPORUM UNDULATUM or VICTORIAN BOX Evergreen tree. Native of Australia.

PRIVET (*Ligustrum*) Evergreen shrub. Needs temperate climate. Native of Japan.

QUEEN ANNE'S LACE (*Daucus carota*) Annual herb. Native of North America.

RANUNCULUS (*Ranunculus asiaticus*) Not hardy. Tuber. Native of southeastern Europe, Syria, and Iran.

ROSEMARY (*Rosmarinus officinalis*) Hardy evergreen perennial herb. Native of southern France.

SNOWFLAKE (*Leucojum vernum*) Hardy bulb. Native of central Europe.

STAR JASMINE (*Trachelospermum jasminoides*) Evergreen vine. Hardy in warm climates. Native of the Himalayas.

SWEET PEAS (*Lathgrus odoratus*) Annual vine grown across the United States. Native of Sicily.

TANGERINE (*Citrus nobilis deliciosa*) Tropical and subtropical evergreen fruit tree. Native of China and India.

TERNSTROEMIA (*Ternstroemia gymnanthera japonica*) Hardy evergreen shrub. Native of tropical America.

TEXAS PRIVET (*Ligustrum*) Evergreen shrub. Not hardy in north. Native of Japan.

TORCH LILY or RED-HOT POKER (*Tritoma*) Hardy perennial herb. Native of Africa.

TULIP (*Tulipa*) Bulb. Introduced into Europe from Turkey.

VIBURNUM or SNOWBALL (*Viburnum opulus roseum*)
Deciduous shrub. Native of Europe.

(*Viburnum suspensum*) Hardy evergreen shrub.
Native of Japan.

(*Viburnum tinus robustum*) Hardy evergreen shrub.
Native of southeastern Europe.

VIOLET (*Viola odorata*) Perennial native of North America.

WISTERIA (*Wistaria sinensis*) Deciduous vine. Native of
China.

YELLOW JASMINE (*Jasminum floridum*) Hardy, evergreen
shrub. Native of China.

YERBA BUENA (*Micromeria chamissonias*) Perennial herb.
Native of the Pacific Coast.

32

*Flower
Arrangements
to Copy*

Green tones

CONTAINERS: A square black ceramic temple vase, 6¼ inches tall and 5 inches wide.
Japanese black lacquered soup bowl, 4¾ inches in diameter.

HOLDERS: A medium-sized kenzan to the left rear of the temple vase, and a small kenzan in the soup bowl.

MATERIALS: Pale greenish-white tristis, spuria-iris leaves, and nutmeg geranium leaves.

BASE: Four black rectangular plateaus, the largest 14 by 10 inches.

COMMENT: Split arrangement: the dominant section arranged in the temple vase and the subordinate section in the soup bowl.

Windblown bamboo

CONTAINER: An oval gold-brown ceramic boat, 16 inches long.

HOLDER: A large kenzan, centered.

MATERIALS: Golden bamboo, yellow daylilies, and meadow silk grass.
A green ceramic frog.

COMMENT: Windblown bamboo kept in balance, optically, by the opposite pull of the daylilies and grasses. Enjoy this arrangement for many days as the daylily buds open, and watch that the frog doesn't leap onto the bamboo.

Fruit and flower centerpiece

CONTAINER: A tiered crystal epergne, 20 inches tall.

HOLDERS: The top vase has a block of oasis.
The lower bowl has five small kenzans.

MATERIALS: Purple-acacia sprigs, pink roses, pink petunias, muscat grapes, and rosy apples.
Pink glass chips.

COMMENT: The block of oasis is held in place by a stick that goes through the oasis down into the vase. Glass chips hide the stick and the kenzans in the lower bowl.

Dramatic catalpa

CONTAINER: A drip-glazed stoneware vase, 13½ inches tall.

HOLDER: A cross stick wired on the largest catalpa branch.

MATERIALS: Branches of catalpa in bloom, bronze New Zealand flax, and red roses.
An elephant figurine.

BASE: A wood burl slab.

COMMENT: Jungle atmosphere.

Quiet elegance

CONTAINER: An olive-green lacquered bowl, 12¾ inches in diameter.

HOLDER: A large kenzan, centered.

MATERIALS: Lavender-blue Japanese iris, blue violas, and spuria-iris leaves.
Light green glass chips.

BASE: A round black teak stand.

Desert in bloom

CONTAINER: The wood slabs are both container and base.

HOLDER: A small cup holder.

MATERIALS: Green succulents with yellow blossoms, red-orange kalanchoe, red-orange sparaxis, and spuria-iris leaves.
Three brown ceramic rabbits.

BASE: Three wood burl slabs.

COMMENT: A stratified mesa is created by stacking the wood slabs.

Tropical poinciana

CONTAINER: A ceramic platter in a brown matte glaze, 16½ inches wide.

HOLDERS: A large kenzan in the left rear, and a medium-sized kenzan in the right foreground.

MATERIALS: Poinciana blossoms, bronze flax leaves, yellow Transvaal daisies, and yellow-orange nasturtiums.

COMMENT: Place this arrangement on a large round table.

Tropical plants

CONTAINER: A green ceramic bowl, 15½ inches in diameter.

HOLDER: A large kenzan, centered.

MATERIALS: An orange and blue bird-of-paradise bloom, New Zealand flax leaves, and aralia leaves.

BASE: A round black teak stand.

COMMENT: Since there were no bird-of-paradise leaves available, the substituted foliage establishes the proper setting for the blossom.

The first peach

CONTAINER: A square beige stoneware bud vase, 9 inches tall.

MATERIALS: A fruit-bearing branch from a peach tree, statice foliage, and moraea-iris leaves.

BASE: A wood burl slab.

COMMENT: No special control is needed. All stems are balanced within the small opening of the container.

Simple effectiveness

CONTAINER: A gold-brown plastic basket, 11 inches in diameter.

HOLDER: A medium-sized kenzan, centered.

MATERIALS: Yellow Iceland poppies and francoa leaves.

BASE: A bamboo raft.

COMMENT: Poppy leaves are so delicate—substitute leaves are used.

50

Winter breakthrough

CONTAINER: A round green stoneware bowl, 11 inches in diameter.

HOLDER: A large kenzan, placed to the left rear.

MATERIALS: Early spring branch of black alder, orange Transvaal daisies with their leaves, and spuria-iris leaves.

BASE: A bamboo raft.

COMMENT: A branch of deciduous alder can be forced to leaf indoors.

Pink clouds

CONTAINER: A glass bowl, 12½ inches in diameter.

HOLDER: A large kenzan, centered.

MATERIALS: Branches of pink flowering raphiolepis, blue scilla, blue agathea, and saxifrage.

54

Royal-blue iris

CONTAINER: A royal-blue ceramic vase, 8½ inches tall.

HOLDERS: Cross sticks.

MATERIALS: Blue Dutch iris, a branch of *pittosporum crassifolium* in bloom, and clusters of daylily foliage.

BASE: A round black teak stand.

COMMENT: Bind the stems of the three irises together before placing them in the vase.

The fleeting moraea-iris blossoms

CONTAINER: A brown and gray stoneware sake jug, 13½ inches tall.

HOLDER: None. The small opening of the jug keeps the stems in place.

MATERIALS: Moraea-iris blossoms and leaves and pepper-mint-geranium leaves.

BASE: A wood burl slab.

COMMENT: Cut and arrange the irises while they are in bud and enjoy the beauty of their opening though it be only for a day.

58

Pink amaryllis

CONTAINER: A low glass bowl, 12½ inches in diameter.

HOLDER: A large kenzan, centered.

MATERIALS: Five stems of pink amaryllis, bronze flax leaves, and saxifrage leaves.
Yellow-green glass chips.

COMMENT: Amaryllis have a mind of their own. They twist and turn both to the light and against their own weight—enjoy their beauty with each change.

60

Autumn air

CONTAINER:	A square brown ceramic dish, 10 inches wide.
HOLDER:	A kenzan, centered.
MATERIALS:	Twisted juniper, gold daisy chrysanthemums, and dried watsonia leaves. A pair of brown ceramic quail.
BASE:	Bamboo rafts.
COMMENT:	Naturally dried watsonia leaves possess interesting twists and warm colors.

62

Quiet pond

CONTAINER: A flat-bottomed green ceramic vessel, 21 by 13½ inches.

HOLDERS: A large kenzan to the left rear, a small ken-zan in the right foreground, and three small kenzans placed to broaden the area of the left large kenzan.

MATERIALS: A branch of pyracantha, snowflake blossoms, spuria-iris foliage, and pink clover blossoms. Flat water-washed rocks of different sizes. Ceramic ducks.

BASE: A large wood burl slab.

COMMENT: Stones add much to the scenic atmosphere.

What do the sparrows see?

CONTAINER: An oval white china dish, 10 inches long.

HOLDER: A medium-sized kenzan, centered.

MATERIALS: Pink baby gladiolus, Esther Reed daisies, white candytuft, and short sprays of flowering-almond foliage.
Two white china sparrows.

BASE: A set of four black plateaus.

COMMENT: Placing flowers to the rear side of this design turns it into a lovely centerpiece.

Tropical buffet

CONTAINER: A wood burl slab, 18 inches long.

HOLDER: A large cup holder, set to the left of the pineapple.

MATERIALS: Orange Transvaal daisies, three aralia leaves, and yellow succulent flowers.
Three brass and amber-glass candleholders of different heights.
Three hand-rolled beeswax candles.
A pineapple.

Exuberant daffodils

CONTAINER: A pineapple-colored oval bowl, 14 inches long.

HOLDER: A large kenzan, centered.

MATERIAL: King Alfred daffodils and their leaves.

BASE: A single bamboo raft.

70

Dangling beauty

CONTAINER: An olive-green lacquered bowl, 12¾ inches in diameter.

HOLDER: A large kenzan, centered.

MATERIALS: Checkerboard fuchsia, asparagus vine, and dahlias of the same color as the centers of the fuchsias.

COMMENT: Fuchsia stems are easy to reshape.

Freshness without water

CONTAINER: None—the arrangement is made directly on the base.

HOLDER: A large kenzan, secured to the base with floral clay.

MATERIALS: Three varieties of rose-tinged succulents and a defoliated branch.

BASE: A set of three rectangular plateaus, the largest 14 by 10 inches.

COMMENT: A good winter arrangement. After a month or so, replant the succulents in your garden.

Summer glory

CONTAINER: An oval green ceramic vessel, 19 inches long.

HOLDER: A large kenzan, centered.

MATERIALS: Orange-yellow loquat fruit and branches, an orange rose, and yellow Spanish broom.

COMMENT: Delicacy and substance combined tell a story.

Preserved eucalyptus

CONTAINER: A patterned white and brown ceramic vase, 9 inches tall.

HOLDER: Styrofoam pack.

MATERIALS: Gray-brown glycerinized spiral eucalyptus, dried lunaria, and dried red cockscomb.

Abundant harvest

CONTAINER: A wood burl slab, 26 inches long.

HOLDERS: A large cup holder for the chrysanthemums. Three heavy kenzans for the wheat shocks.

MATERIALS: Bearded wheat (3 dozen heads to each shock), Burgundy-colored chrysanthemums, dried watsonia leaves, and autumn-tinged geranium leaves.
Three table-queen squashes.
Emperor grapes.
Assorted nuts.
Yellow crookneck squashes.

COMMENT: Use floral clay to stabilize squashes.

Curved calla lilies

CONTAINER: A glass bowl, 13 inches in diameter.

HOLDER: A large kenzan, centered.

MATERIALS: Seven white calla lilies and five leaves with white candytuft.

COMMENT: Calla-lily stems are curved by gripping them and drawing the stem into the desired curve.

Glorified gloriosa

CONTAINER: A shallow round matte-brown ceramic bowl, 12 inches in diameter.

HOLDER: A large kenzan, centered.

MATERIALS: A gloriosa daisy, francoa leaves, meadow silk grass, and defoliated twigs.

BASE: Kiri-wood raft.

COMMENT: The delicacy of the meadow silk grass and the twists of the bare twigs accentuate the strength and character of the daisy.

Midsummer scene

CONTAINER: A rectangular platter in a pale green matte glaze, 21 by 13¾ inches.

HOLDERS: A large kenzan and a small kenzan.

MATERIALS: Branches of strawberry guava and twigs of correa.
Ceramic deer.
Rocks.

COMMENT: Lush midsummer foliage creates a cool setting for a family of deer.

New shoots

CONTAINER: A tiered gold candy dish, 7 inches square, with red-orange lining.

HOLDERS: A medium-sized kenzan and a small kenzan.

MATERIALS: A new shoot of asparagus fern, moraea-iris leaves, and Indian Chief begonia.

BASE: Bamboo rafts.

COMMENT: Stabilize the stacked containers with small bits of floral clay or stickum at points of contact.

84

Cool brightness

CONTAINER: A green ceramic bowl, 15½ inches in diameter.

HOLDER: A large kenzan, centered.

MATERIALS: Golden bamboo, variegated New Zealand flax, and orange seedling dahlias.

BASE: A wood burl slab.

Vegetables are flowers too!

CONTAINER: A wicker bread basket, 22½ inches long (including handles).

HOLDER: A large cup holder.

MATERIALS: Newly formed seed heads of parsley, stalks of celery, orange dahlias, and red-brown-tipped succulents.

COMMENT: Brunch is in order.

Hand-shucked pussy willows

CONTAINER: A pale green ceramic compote, 6½ inches tall.

HOLDER: A medium-sized kenzan, centered.

MATERIALS: Pussy willows, blue Dutch iris, a yellow Transvaal daisy, and red-tinged Transvaal-daisy leaves.

BASE: A wood burl slab.

COMMENT: Gather pussy willows before they burst their shells. Peel away shells to expose the catkins.

90

A crisscross design

CONTAINER: An oval gold-brown ceramic bowl, 16 inches long.

HOLDER: A large kenzan, centered.

MATERIALS: Bronze bearded iris, purple-leaf plum, and ornamental geranium.

COMMENT: Only a single stem of this hybrid iris was picked. The lower blossom was originally attached to the main stem.

92

Charming

CONTAINER: A pale green cutout vase, 11½ inches tall.

HOLDER: A large kenzan.

MATERIALS: White flowering-almond branches and yellow innominata irises and their leaves.

COMMENT: The cutout container ensures three-dimensional designs.

Autumn lavender

CONTAINER: A white-ware relish dish, 10 inches long.

HOLDER: A medium-sized kenzan.

MATERIALS: Lavender spider chrysanthemums, cerise scabiosa, and saxifrage leaves.
A pair of white china pheasants.

BASE: A black scroll stand.

Christmas "lites"

CONTAINER: A gold-leafed tray, 14½ inches in diameter.

HOLDERS: A medium-sized kenzan to the left of the tall candle.
Three small kenzans: one in front of the tall candle, one to the left of the medium candle, and one to the right front of the short candle.

MATERIALS: Monterey pine, English holly, and pine cones.
Three green bayberry candles. The tallest is 12 inches high, the medium is 9 inches, and the short one is 6 inches.
Three large red Christmas-tree ornaments and one extra-large ornament.
Stemmed red ornaments of assorted sizes.
Curls of coat-hanger wire wrapped with gold tinsel ribbon.

COMMENT: To form the curls, first straighten the coat hanger and wrap it with floral tape; then wrap it with gold ribbon and bend it to the desired shape. To anchor the curl in the kenzan, attach a piece of fresh woody stem or place it in a short section of bamboo. Place the curls so that the ornaments fall free of the flame.

A lone iris

CONTAINER: A yellow-green ceramic compote, 6½ inches
            high.

HOLDER: A large kenzan, centered.

MATERIALS: A bronze-colored bearded iris and a branch
            of myrtle.
            Pale green glass slag in assorted sizes.

COMMENT: This iris had a short stem but was too hand-
            some not to be arranged. Using a compote
            helps to offset the lack of stem length.

That one camellia

CONTAINER: A smoked crystal salad bowl, 7 inches in diameter.

HOLDER: A small kenzan, centered.

MATERIALS: A pink camellia and its foliage and a curly defoliated twig from a pomegranate tree. Clear glass slag in assorted sizes.

BASE: Three round black plateaus.

COMMENT: Simplicity allows complete enjoyment of the camellia's perfection.

Wild flowers in a basket LOWER ARRANGEMENT

CONTAINER: A wicker basket, 12 inches long.

HOLDER: A large cup holder.

MATERIALS: Yellow marguerites, yellow gaillardia, and rose-pink gilla.

COMMENT: The lushness of early spring. Enjoy it!

Three gladiolus

CONTAINER: An oval black dish, 19 inches long.

HOLDER: A large kenzan, centered.

MATERIALS: Three pink gladiolus, spuria-iris leaves, and pink-tinged gerbera leaves.

COMMENT: Angle the shortest gladiolus forward to ensure depth in the arrangement.

Peaceful union

CONTAINER: A white stoneware sunabachi, 11¼ inches square.

HOLDERS: A large kenzan in front of the Madonna, a small kenzan in the left foreground, and a small kenzan in the right rear corner.

MATERIALS: Yellow moraea iris, white gladiolus tips and blossoms, and Algerian ivy leaves.

COMMENT: Used this way, the large blossom of the gladiolus becomes subordinated to the Madonna.

104

Cymbidiums

CONTAINER: A green stoneware suiban, 12½ inches in diameter.

HOLDER: A large kenzan, centered.

MATERIALS: Branches of purple-leaf plum, a spike of green cymbidiums and leaves, and ornamental geranium.

BASE: Bamboo rafts.

Spectacular begonia

CONTAINER: A beige stoneware compote, 12 inches across.

HOLDER: A large kenzan, centered.

MATERIALS: Angel-wing begonia, Australian brake fern, and moraea-iris leaves.

BASE: A kiri-wood raft.

COMMENT: How beautifully Nature designed this begonia.

Naturally abstract

CONTAINER:	A twisted brown Bizen-ware vase, 10½ inches high.
HOLDER:	None. Stems are naturally braced within the vase.
MATERIALS:	A red-orange Mexican orchid, moraea-iris leaves, and three catalpa-tree leaves.
BASE:	A wood burl slab.
COMMENT:	Prearrange iris leaves and wire or tape them together before placing them in the vase.

110

Elegant magnolia

CONTAINER: A green lacquered fruit bowl, 12¾ inches in diameter.

HOLDER: A kenzan, centered.

MATERIALS: Magnolias, meadow silk grass, and saxifrage leaves.

BASE: A round black teakwood stand.

COMMENT: Simple, but commands attention.

112

Set a bright table

CONTAINER: A black lacquered fruit bowl, 12¾ inches in diameter.

HOLDER: A large kenzan, centered.

MATERIALS: Three stems of yellow gladiolus, twelve bananas, six lemons, and Algerian-ivy leaves.
Four brass candlesticks.
Four 15-inch hand-rolled yellow beeswax candles.

COMMENT: Begin this design by arranging the ivy leaves. Shorten the gladiolus stems and use just the tips and blossoms. Upright bananas are impaled on the needles of the kenzan; the others are balanced on the bowl. Ivy leaves will last for several days out of water.

114

Typically Hawaiian

CONTAINER: A flat-bottomed brown ceramic tray, 13½ inches in diameter.

HOLDER: A cup holder.

MATERIALS: Orange butterfly gladiolus, aralia leaves, orange Transvaal daisies, and spuria-iris foliage.
Coco sticks.
A fresh pineapple.

COMMENT: A party arrangement created with butterfly-gladiolus blooms pierced by coco sticks and stuck between the pineapple leaves. The other materials are secured in the cup holder behind the pineapple. Fresh gladiolus blossoms will stay firm for two days without water. Mist with water to assure crispness.

116

Look to your herbs

CONTAINERS: Two white stoneware sunabachis. The bottom one measures 13½ by 5 inches. The upper one measures 11 by 4½ inches.

HOLDERS: Two kenzans in the top container, and one small kenzan in the lower container.

MATERIALS: Francoa blossoms and foliage, flowering-almond branches, Esther Reed daisies, leaves and blossoms from a Chinese garlic plant.

BASE: Two driftwood slats.

COMMENT: Delicate flower forms have been given substance by being arranged in heavy solid containers. Stabilize the stacked containers with small bits of floral clay or stickum at points of contact.

118

Solitude

CONTAINER: An oval bowl in a light green matte glaze, 19 inches long.

HOLDER: A large kenzan, centered.

MATERIALS: Blue lily-of-the-Nile, its leaves, and aspidistra foliage.

COMMENT: Let this arrangement speak for itself.

120

Shady stream

CONTAINER: A white stoneware suiban, 16¼ by 9¼ inches.

HOLDERS: A large kenzan in the right rear, a small kenzan in the front center, and a small kenzan in the left center.

MATERIALS: Branches of catalpa tree in bloom, Esther Reed daisies, King Henry violas, and a clump of liriope leaves.

BASE: Driftwood slats.

Our first tiger lily

CONTAINER: An orange-lined gold-leafed candy bowl.

HOLDER: A kenzan, centered.

MATERIALS: A stalk of orange tiger lily, moraea-iris leaves,
              and ornamental-geranium leaves.
              An orange fish of woven bamboo.

BASE: A gold-leafed tray, 15 inches in diameter.

COMMENT: A subtle combination of elegant and common
              textures in which the tiger lily is at ease.

124

Captured summer mood

CONTAINER: A shallow, rectangular white stoneware suna-bachi, 9 by 16 inches.

HOLDERS: Five small kenzans.

MATERIALS: Meadow silk grass, blue agathea, pink fairy roses, spuria-iris leaves, umbrella plant, and bush morning-glory foliage.
A white porcelain lantern, 4½ inches tall.
Green glass chips.

COMMENT: Green glass chips have been used to simulate a green ground cover and to outline the banks of the stream. Refreshing!

126

Early spring calla lilies

CONTAINER: A green stoneware compote, 12 inches in diameter.

HOLDER: A large kenzan, centered.

MATERIALS: A loquat branch bursting with new growth, two calla lilies with their leaves, and spuria-iris foliage.

BASE: A large wood burl slab.

COMMENT: This arrangement holds the promise of an abundant spring.

128

Serene bull

CONTAINER: None.

HOLDER: A large cup holder.

MATERIALS: A Bizen-ware bull.
Day lily stalk carrying new plants, leather-wood fern, moraea-iris leaves, and wild yellow buttercups.

BASE: A kiri-wood raft, 20 inches long.

COMMENT: The tallest stem of fern makes a canopy for the bull.

Winter breakthrough

CONTAINER: A triangular white china dish, 8 inches in diameter.

HOLDER: A small kenzan, centered.

MATERIALS: Spanish broom, snowflakes, and amaryllis leaves.

BASE: A carved round black stand.

COMMENT: Spanish broom is available through your florist.

Mid-summer day lilies

CONTAINER: A white stoneware cylinder, 13¾ inches tall.

HOLDER: None.

MATERIALS: Hybrid day lilies and a short branch of loquat.

BASE: A round plateau.

COMMENT: First, place the stem of loquat in the con-
              tainer. It will reduce the size of the opening
              and form support for the daylily stems. Open
              blossoms show their beauty for only a day,
              but succeeding buds will open to give enjoy-
              ment for a week or more.

134

Summer stillness

CONTAINER: A white stoneware suiban, 16¼ by 9¼ inches.

HOLDER: A large kenzan, anchored to the left side.

MATERIALS: A branch of silver-dollar eucalyptus, orange tiger lilies, meadow silk grass, and liriope leaves.

BASE: A large cedar-wood slab.

COMMENT: Let this arrangement become a living mural against a clear wall area.

Early daffodils

CONTAINER: A green-black ceramic compote, 11 inches in diameter.

HOLDER: A kenzan, centered.

MATERIALS: King Alfred daffodils, amaryllis leaves, and a *Pittosporum rhombilfolium* branch with berries.

BASE: A wood burl slab.

COMMENT: Amaryllis leaves make a splendid substitute for the leafless florist daffodils.

Substitute foliage

CONTAINER: A clear glass bowl, 12 inches in diameter.

HOLDER: A large kenzan, centered.

MATERIALS: Blue agapanthus blossoms, spuria-iris leaves, and leatherwood fern.
Chartreuse green glass chips.

COMMENT: Spuria-iris leaves are used to support the leafless agapanthus stems. The leatherwood fern introduces a texture change and completes the balance of the design.

140

Magnolias

CONTAINER: A large green matte-glazed ceramic bowl, 15¾ inches in diameter.

HOLDER: A large kenzan, centered.

MATERIALS: Magnolia branches bearing blossoms and spuria-iris leaves.

COMMENT: Allow enough space for each magnolia blossom to display itself in all its dramatic beauty.

142

Baby gladiolus

CONTAINER: A white china compote, 9 inches in diameter.

HOLDER: A kenzan, centered.

MATERIALS: Pink baby gladiolus, saxifrage leaves, and liriope leaves.

COMMENT: The round form necessary to all arrangements is introduced by the use of the saxifrage leaves.

Feminity

CONTAINER: A crystal compote, 10½ inches across.

HOLDER: A kenzan, centered.

MATERIALS: Two new shoots of asparagus fern, pink fairy roses, and liriope leaves.

COMMENT: A lovely combination of delicate materials.

Wallflower

CONTAINER: A cutout ceramic vase, glazed pale green, 11½ inches tall.

HOLDER: A kenzan.

MATERIALS: A flowering-almond branch, liriope leaves, and yellow-orange wallflowers.

BASE: A set of three rectangular plateaus.

COMMENT: The simple wallflower takes center stage.

146

Jungle clivia

CONTAINERS: A black ceramic boat, 19 inches long, set
              stern end forward, with a matching ceramic
              compote, 6 inches high, placed to the rear.

HOLDERS: Two medium-sized kenzans.

MATERIALS: Orange clivia blossoms and leaves, spuria-
              iris leaves, orange sparaxis blossoms, and
              loquat leaves.
              A hand-carved crane made from the horn of
              a water buffalo.

COMMENT: The shortness of the clivia stem is overcome
              by placing it in the compote.

148

Simplicity with variety

CONTAINER: A blue ceramic bowl, 13 inches in diameter.

HOLDER: A large kenzan, centered.

MATERIALS: A pink flowering-peach branch, blue Dutch iris, blue agathea, and pink dianthus.

COMMENT: Just one iris is purposely used to maintain interest and balance of color.

Ring in the new year

CONTAINER: A crystal brandy snifter, 11 inches high.

HOLDER: A heavy large kenzan.

MATERIALS: A cerise-colored rose fully opened (hybrid tea), a stalk of golden bamboo, and liriope leaves.
Three cerise-colored silk bells.
Four pastel-colored party whistles.
Pink food coloring for the water.

COMMENT: Secure the rose and its leaves before arranging the bamboo and liriope leaves. The whistles are tied to the twigs with fine wire.

152

Inquisitive easter bunnies

CONTAINER: A white stoneware suiban, 16 by 9¼ inches.

HOLDERS: Three small kenzans: one to the rear left center, one to the left front, and one to the right-side edge.

MATERIALS: Blue-pink sun azaleas, blue-pink scilla, blue violas, and blue-pink marguerites.
Three white ceramic bunnies.
A black plateau.

BASE: Two black plateaus, 11 and 9 inches in diameter.

154

"Glad" rockets for the 4th

CONTAINER: A rectangular white sunabachi, 16 inches long and 9 inches wide.

HOLDERS: Two small kenzans; one placed in the left rear corner and the other in the right front corner. A large kenzan in the left of center.

MATERIALS: Red-painted cat-tails, red gladiolus, white carnations, and sun-camellia twigs.
Blue food coloring for the water.

COMMENT: Thread gladiolus blossoms over the tips of the cat-tails.

156

Friendly ghoul

CONTAINER: A flat black ceramic platter, 15½ inches in diameter.

HOLDERS: One large kenzan and two small kenzans.

MATERIALS: Catalpa branches bearing seedpods, pineapple-guava twigs, dusty-miller leaves, candelabra succulents, and dried herb stalks.
A ghost made from a pale green balloon with a gray ribbon shroud and suspended on a coco stick.

COMMENT: Blow up a long balloon leaving the tip uninflated. Tie off a portion to make the head of the ghost. Catch various lengths of gray satin ribbon together with wire, forming bangs and shroud effect, and attach to the head with Scotch tape. Pass the coco stick through the knot of the balloon.

158

Autumn berries

CONTAINER: A yellow-green ceramic compote, 6½ inches
              tall and 8 inches in diameter.

HOLDER: A large kenzan, centered.

MATERIALS: A small Japanese rice-paper plant, red-
              orange pyracantha berries, and a yellow
              Transvaal daisy with its red-orange-tipped
              leaves.

BASE: A set of black rectangular plateaus.

COMMENT: The stiffness of the pyracantha stem is soft-
              ened by allowing the paper plant leaf to
              cross its stem.

160

Bumpy gourds

CONTAINER: A yellow-green ceramic compote, 6½ inches tall.

HOLDER: A kenzan, centered.

MATERIALS: Spanish broom, Hahn ivy, French marigolds, succulents, and three orange gourds.

BASE: A black oval plateau, 15 inches long.

162

Pattern of fruit and flowers

CONTAINER: A green and black ceramic compote, 6½ inches high and 10½ inches in diameter.

HOLDER: A large kenzan, centered.

MATERIALS: A stalk of golden bamboo, fruit of the pineapple guava, orange pittosporum berries, yellow spoon chrysanthemums, and moraea-iris leaves.
Fine green wire with which to hang the guavas.

COMMENT: A three-foot-tall arrangement creates a lovely autumn painting against a plain background.

164

Decorative black alder

CONTAINER: A black ceramic cutout vase, 11½ inches tall.

HOLDER: A large kenzan, centered.

MATERIALS: A black-alder branch, yellow spoon chrysanthemums, and day lily leaves.
A hand-carved crane from the horn of a water buffalo.

BASE: Three black oval plateaus, the largest 15 inches long.

COMMENT: The crane complements the water-loving alder and balances the over-all design.

166

Drama from blossomless stalks

CONTAINER: An oval pale yellow-green ceramic bowl, 19 inches long.

HOLDER: An extra-large kenzan, centered.

MATERIALS: Green agapanthus stalks that have finished blooming, bronze flax leaves, and bronze-colored pompon chrysanthemums.

COMMENT: Interest is created by the use of diagonally cut sections of flax stems.

168

Autumn gold

CONTAINER: A sectioned brown plastic candy dish, finished black inside, 8½ inches in diameter.

HOLDER: A medium-sized kenzan.

MATERIALS: Frilly yellow spoon chrysanthemums, browned seed heads and leaves of blue-eyed grass, and variegated-geranium leaves.
A hand-carved toad.

BASE: A kiri-wood raft.

COMMENT: Simple stems are enhanced by the candy-dish cover and the toad.

Waiting the witching hour

CONTAINER: A black ceramic platter, 12 inches in diameter.

HOLDER: A large kenzan, centered.

MATERIALS: Spanish Broom sprayed black, red bell peppers, and loquat leaves.
A balloon witch.

COMMENT: The witch is made of a pale green balloon. The soft balloon tip is her nose. She is attached to a twig of Spanish broom and stabilized by a fine wire from her nose to the broom. Her hair, hat, and cape are made of lengths of black ribbon taped to the balloon. Impale the highest pepper on a twig.

172

Just callas

CONTAINER: A black lacquered bowl, 12¾ inches in diameter.

HOLDER: A large kenzan, centered.

MATERIALS: Calla lilies with their foliage.

BASE: A set of three rectangular black plateaus, the largest 14 by 10 inches.

COMMENT: Calla lilies require no help to show their beauty.

Universal appeal

CONTAINER: A round brown sandstone suiban, 12½ inches in diameter.

HOLDER: A large kenzan, secured on the right side.

MATERIALS: Monterey pine and pink roses.

BASE: Bamboo rafts.

COMMENT: Femininity and masculinity brought together in perfect harmony—invites contemplation.

174

Winter blossoms

CONTAINER: A black lacquered bowl, 13 inches in diameter.

HOLDER: A large kenzan, centered.

MATERIALS: Branch of purple-leaf plum and pink saxifrage blossoms and their leaves.
A crane carved from the horn of a water buffalo.

BASE: A round teak stand and three driftwood slats.

COMMENT: When you see these flowers in bloom, spring is well on its way.

176

The first yellow iris

CONTAINER: A white stoneware sunabachi, 11 inches square.

HOLDERS: Three medium-sized kenzans.

MATERIALS: A yellow bearded iris, yellow violas, and white azaleas.
Yellow-green glass chips.

COMMENT: Glass chips are arranged to simulate a grassy bank. A feeling of abundance captured with so little.

178

Strength

CONTAINER: A round brown ceramic bowl, 17 inches in diameter.

HOLDERS: Two heavy extra-large kenzans placed in line, centered, front and back.

MATERIALS: Giant bamboo, Monterey pine, and yellow spoon chrysanthemums.

BASE: A large wood burl slab.

COMMENT: The giant bamboo has been trimmed severely of excess foliage and twigs. Woody stems have first been secured in the kenzan and the hollow bamboo stems slipped over them for control.

Polar cap

CONTAINER: A black stoneware sunabachi, 11 inches square.

HOLDERS: A large kenzan in the rear left corner, and a tiny kenzan in the front right corner.

MATERIALS: White Chinese garlic blossoms, white scabiosa, dusty-miller leaves, and cress foliage.
White china penguins.
Black water-washed rocks.

BASE: Three round black plateaus.

COMMENT: Summer at the South Pole.

Colors of autumn

CONTAINER: A brown stoneware compote, 8 inches in diameter.

HOLDER: A medium-sized kenzan.

MATERIALS: Gold plumed celosia, bronze pompon chrysanthemums, and reddish-brown barberry twigs.

BASE: A bamboo raft.

Simplicity

CONTAINERS: Three rectangular white stoneware vessels, two measuring 18½ inches long and 4½ inches wide, and one measuring 11½ by 4½.

HOLDERS: Three medium-sized kenzans.

MATERIALS: White bearded irises and yellow innominata irises.

COMMENT: The open spacing gives room to the magnificent irises for greater enjoyment.

186

Autumn buffet

CONTAINER: A 12-inch glass plate with gold-plated candle holder attached.

HOLDER: A kenzan in the rear and a kenzan in the front.

MATERIALS: Dried sea-oats, bittersweet, succulents, and red natal-plum fruit on twigs.
Amber glass chips.

COMMENT: This arrangement requires no water. Kenzans are hidden by glass chips.

From the produce counter

CONTAINER: An oval pale yellow-green ceramic bowl, 19 inches long.

HOLDER: An extra-large kenzan, centered.

MATERIALS: An opened artichoke, yellow chili peppers, and variegated New Zealand flax leaves.

BASE: A black scroll stand.

COMMENT: The brown-tipped flax leaves were purposely shredded. Open the artichoke by hand by folding out each petal. To do this, keep the artichoke at room temperature. The peppers were clustered together with wire. Peppers used high in the arrangement were pierced onto sticks.

Duck blind

CONTAINER: A rectangular green stoneware sunabachi, 16 by 9 inches.

HOLDERS: Three kenzans.

MATERIALS: Equisetum, Australian brake fern, and aralia flowers.
A pair of mallard ducks.

BASE: Bamboo rafts.

COMMENT: A masculine centerpiece.

192

Trick or treat

CONTAINERS: A black plastic tray, 18 inches in diameter. A black disc, 11 inches in diameter. A square black ceramic vase, 8 inches high.

HOLDER: A large cup holder in the tray in front of the square vase.

MATERIALS: A pumpkin, pinwheel gloriosa daisies, loquat leaves, and ornamental gourds.
Jelly beans on coco sticks.
Trick-or-treat candy packets.
Orange and black satin ribbon.
Three brass candle holders and three orange candles.

COMMENT: The face of the jack o'lantern is made with black ribbon pinned into place. Loquat-leaf hair is made by piercing the leaves directly into the pumpkin—use ice pick or knife to cut skin. Bags of candy are pinned to the orange ribbon loops.

194

Happy chickadees

CONTAINER: A green stoneware sunabachi, 16 inches long and 9 inches wide.

HOLDERS: One large kenzan and one small kenzan.

MATERIALS: Branches of newly foliated saucer magnolia, gold innominata iris, yellow gaillardia, and a twig of lemon in bloom.
Three ceramic chickadees.
Stones and pebbles.

BASE: Three driftwood slats.

COMMENT: The chickadee in the container is sitting on a flat rock.

196

Tall dried arrangement

CONTAINER: A hand-fashioned stoneware vase.

HOLDER: Styrofoam pack.

MATERIALS: Black-brown New Zealand flax seedpods, gray-brown glycerinized spiral eucalyptus, and gold dried yarrow.

COMMENT: A hearthside arrangement for year-round enjoyment.

Miniature gladiolus

CONTAINER: A pale yellow-green ceramic cutout vase, 11½ inches tall.

HOLDER: A large kenzan.

MATERIALS: Yellow-green gladiolus and narcissus leaves. A green ceramic frog.

BASE: Three round plateaus, the largest 11 inches in diameter.

COMMENT: Gladiolus leaves are so thin—adding the narcissus leaves complements nicely.

Cheeseboard arrangement

CONTAINER: A small oval glass bowl on a cheeseboard.

HOLDER: A medium-sized kenzan.

MATERIALS: Quaking grass, Chinese garlic seed heads, and leatherwood fern.
Summer squash, an off-white squash, and green grapes.

BASE: A cheeseboard, 12 inches square.

COMMENT: The summer squash is projected on a stick.

A perfect rose

CONTAINER: A green lacquered bowl, 13 inches in diameter.

HOLDER: A large kenzan, centered.

MATERIALS: A specimen pink rose and loquat leaves.

COMMENT: Enjoy this single rose without distraction.

An intriguing container

CONTAINER: A hanging ceramic ashtray in a green-black glaze, 6 inches in diameter and 7 inches high.

HOLDER: A medium-sized kenzan.

MATERIALS: A horizontal branch of sun camellia, yellow chrysanthemums, and moraea-iris leaves.
A green ceramic frog.

BASE: A black scroll stand.

COMMENT: A side branch angles out happily from this unusual container.

206

Fragrant foliage and flowers

CONTAINER: A round green ceramic bowl, 7 inches in diameter.

HOLDER: A large kenzan, centered.

MATERIALS: Pink roses, spiral eucalyptus, and lavender-pink fountain grass.

COMMENT: Pink and gray-greens are pleasant together.

Patio arrangement

CONTAINER: A wooden wheelbarrow, 4 inches high, 14 inches long, and with a barrow 9½ inches in diameter.

HOLDER: A large cup holder.

MATERIALS: Meadow silk grass, French marigolds, gold chrysanthemums, ornamental-geranium foliage, and liriope leaves.

COMMENT: A wheelbarrow full of color.

210

High-low

CONTAINERS: A square white stoneware suiban, 12 inches wide, and a square white stoneware vase, 9 inches tall and 3 inches wide.

HOLDERS: Three-quarters of the tall vase is filled with clean sand, and a heavy lead-based kenzan set on top of the sand. Two medium-sized kenzans in the suiban.

MATERIALS: Balloon-vine, equisetum, maidenhair fern, and yellow chrysanthemums.
A dried defoliated twig.
Two ceramic mallard ducks.

COMMENT: Anchor the twig in the kenzan and then twine the vine around it. Be sure to burn the stems of the fern and harden before arranging.

212

Valentine flowers

CONTAINER: A white china compote, 10 inches in diameter.

HOLDER: A large kenzan, centered.

MATERIALS: Red roses, white alyssum, and moraea-iris leaves.

BASE: A black disc, 9 inches in diameter.

214

Spider lily

CONTAINER: An amber crystal compote, 8½ inches in diameter.

HOLDER: A medium-sized kenzan.

MATERIALS: A yellow-gold spider lily, moraea-iris leaves, and peppermint-geranium leaves.

COMMENT: This lily blooms after its leaves have faded.

216

Spring loveliness

CONTAINER: A crystal compote, 10½ inches in diameter.

HOLDER: A large kenzan.

MATERIALS: Pink flowering peach twigs, blue scilla, white alyssum, and pink Lady Washington geraniums.
Green glass chips.

218

Charming fuchsias

CONTAINER: A green ceramic vase, with turquoise over-glaze, 11 inches high.

HOLDER: None. Stems support each other in the small opening.

MATERIALS: Pink fuchsias, moraea-iris leaves, and dusty-miller foliage.

BASE: A black teak stand.

COMMENT: The bud vase allows the fuchsias to dangle gracefully.

220

Petite designs

TOP DESIGN

CONTAINER: A stoneware "rock" vase, with several open-
ings.

HOLDER: A tiny kenzan.

MATERIALS: Meadow silk grass, French marigolds, and
succulents.

COMMENT: Impale the silk-grass stem on the tiny kenzan, then lower it through one small opening.

LOWER DESIGN

CONTAINER: A crystal sherbert dish, 4½ inches in diameter.

HOLDER: A small kenzan.

MATERIALS: Ruffled petunias and spuria-iris leaves.

BASE: A black scroll stand.

222

Orange accent

CONTAINER: An orange-colored china rice bowl, 4½ inches in diameter.

HOLDER: A small kenzan.

MATERIAL: Angel-wing begonia, leatherwood fern, and liriope leaves.

BASE: A round black disc, 5½ inches in diameter.

224

Harmony

CONTAINER:	A brown Bizen-ware bucket, 6 inches high and 6 inches wide.
HOLDER:	A small kenzan.
MATERIAL:	A specimen daffodil and its leaves.
BASE:	A wood burl slab.

226

Daffodils with young foliage

CONTAINER: A brown and green ceramic compote, 12 inches in diameter.

HOLDER: A large kenzan.

MATERIALS: Branches of saucer magnolia showing fresh spring foliage, cream daffodils, and ornamental-geranium leaves.

228

Pineapple guava in bloom

CONTAINER: A green stoneware sunabachi, 16 by 10 inches.

HOLDERS: A medium-sized kenzan and a small kenzan.

MATERIALS: A pineapple-guava branch, red Indian Chief begonia, and dusty-miller buds and leaves.

230

Pink centerpiece

CONTAINERS: A crystal epergne, 14 inches tall and 10 inches in diameter, set in a small glass dish.

HOLDER: A block of oasis in the top vase.

MATERIALS: Pink roses, pink camellias, and pink escallonia blossoms.
Green glass chips.

COMMENT: Tea-table centerpiece.

Spring pink

CONTAINER: A boat-shaped blue-green ceramic bowl, 14 inches long.

HOLDER: A large kenzan, centered.

MATERIALS: Pink Transvaal daisies and leaves, rose geranium in bloom, pink sun azalea, and daffodil leaves.

BASE: A wood burl slab.

COMMENT: A monochromatic use of pink.

Index